The
Life
of
Me

ORLANDO ELLIS-MOORE

Copyright © 2024 by Orlando Ellis-Moore.

All rights reserved. No part of this publication may be reproduced, distributed, or transmitted in any form or by any means, including photocopying, recording, or other electronic or mechanical methods, without the written consent of the publisher. The only exceptions are for brief quotations included in critical reviews and other noncommercial uses permitted by copyright law.

MILTON & HUGO L.L.C.
4407-11 Park Ave., Suite 5
Union City, NJ 07087, USA

Website: *www.miltonandhugo.com*
Hotline: *1- 888-778-0033*
Email: *info@miltonandhugo.com*

Ordering Information:
Quantity sales. Special discounts are granted to corporations, associations, and other organizations. For more information on these discounts, please reach out to the publisher using the contact information provided above.

Library of Congress Control Number:	IN-PROCESS
ISBN-13: 979-8-89285-008-7	[Paperback Edition]
979-8-89285-009-4	[Hardback Edition]
979-8-89285-010-0	[Digital Edition]

Rev. date: 02/05/2024

Based on a true story

"Finding your purpose is keen to enjoying the happiness you desire".

– Orlando Ellis-Moore

CONTENTS

Chapter 1 My Thoughts 1
Chapter 2 Jail 9
Chapter 3 Relationships 13
Chapter 4 To My Children 15
Chapter 5 Forgiveness 19
Chapter 6 Letting Go and Moving On 23
Chapter 7 A Newer Me 27
              Part One 27
              Part Two 31
Chapter 8 Family 35

CHAPTER 1

MY THOUGHTS

If you were in my shoes how long would you last? Would you quit? Would you let the enemy win? Or would you want to un-alive yourself? To tell you the truth I can barely last in my own shoes. I tried… I tried to give into those same questions previously asked, but I failed. I Failed so badly that it caused me more pain than when I lost. Rather it be in life, love, friendships, as a sibling, or even as a son… Something that I intentionally left out was the streets. As the saying goes "The streets don't love nobody" which is true to a certain extent but the reality is, the streets is cold but its fair. Jump in the water with the sharks it's eat or get ate, same goes for "Jumping off the porch". It's not for everyone especially if you didn't have an upbringing like myself an those of my peers you didn't have to be "street". But just like life the streets has its consequences innocent or not.

I'm in jail right now writing this with my brother in the next block over, in and out of the system constantly. My sister fighting for her life at the hospital level 4 ICU, and watching my oldest sister working hard for the life she wants and deserves but she feels like I blame her for not listening to me moments before leading up to my arrest. My mom is trying her best to stay strong for all of her kids but rent is due. Real life sets in every time she stops her own for the sake of others.

So let me ask you again. If you were in my shoes would you fold? What about when it comes to kids, when you have women playing with your mentality, and emotions as if the child is yours, would you fold? What about if your whole life you have been humble, unselfish and would do anything for those of whom you love and still be envied, hated, betrayed, let down and heartbroken… WOULD YOU FOLD!?

It's almost biblical how my life has played out and just like those in the Bible… I DID NOT FOLD! Not in the interrogation room, not in life, not in anything. So why would I fold now? That thought hasn't crossed my mind in years. Do you want to know why? Because of that man above, God.

I always felt like the black sheep of the family but now I know that I am chosen. Chosen! Can you believe that? Me chosen out of all people, God told me I'm chosen. Chosen to be the best man, the best father, the best son and the best educator to those that are in need of guidance like I did growing up.

I'm at peace now more than I ever have been in my life. That's crazy to say right? I'm literally incarcerated right now saying that I'm more at peace than I have ever been in my entire life. The difference between then and now is that I've had short bursts of real love and real peace over the course of my life and now I can say I have achieved a new milestone or as scripture would say I've had a breakthrough to know that better is coming.

I'm not saying jail is peaceful, it's jail. I still got "opp's" (opposition), I still get unknown hate, I'm still treated like a criminal and I still have my days to were I want to "bug up" or "crash out". If I told you how I got here you wouldn't blame me if I did, as a matter of fact you would want to do it for me If I told you who put me here.

But it's okay. I understand why that person did what they did. That person felt how I felt growing up… betrayed, heartbroken, and left alone in a world when all they wanted to was to be loved… they just went about it in the wrong way. They sought-after revenge instead of forgiveness, they chose to do things out of spite instead of love and tried to play God when there is only one true God that controls judgement day and just because that person felt that way doesn't make it right but I UNDERSTAND!.

I understand why they did what they did, I understand why women want me to be the father, I understand why my "opp's" hate me, I understand why my 10 year homie has slowly fell back from me over time, I UNDERSTAND!. And just because I understand, is the exact reason why there won't be a misunderstanding on my end.

So yes I can truly say I'm at peace. This is not one of those were I got into some type of trouble and ran to God. Before this I was going to church every Sunday and working for the city throughout the week. On my leisure time I would still write music, read the bible, and listening to Christian music more than rap, while doing as a man should, handling his known responsibilities all the while making my family proud of this newly profound me.

Everyday I wake up in this cell, I wake up strong in prayer same as I do before I go to sleep. If I wrote down every thought and every dream I've ever had since I've been here I don't think they would have enough paper throughout this whole side of the facility.

Some would move you, some would inspire you, and some you would be ashamed of if you knew or better yet disappointed. But I'm still human, still a child of God, fighting sin and the spirit of evil everyday. From this point on I will tell you about my good dreams.

My dream started off with me at home picking out a decent outfit and looking through the fridge full of food and snacks off of link. It's some spaghetti in there and DC young fly wanted me to eat some while rushing me out of the door so I can make it in time for the half time show.

I was under the impression that I would be watching it… they had me as the top artist performing, In front of the same people I grew up with and had issues with.

As I was walking through I saw "little dude" from the club and everybody else that I used to be friends with yapping at the mouth like I won't steal off of every last one of them and go straight back to what I was doing. But through the grace of God, I know that he wants us to be slow to anger. So I continue to stay focused on what I'm doing.

Little did I know they started asking me the same questions as the surprise interviewer DC hooked me up with. Which was why did I quit football? I answered stating that "I wanted to pursue music". And they were mad, they envied and hated me just like they did before but this time it paid off because I was the main act of the show.

That's what I like about my dreams. I would always be with the stars and famous people 24/7 and on tour with my favorite artist Rod Wave and more. That's how I know I'm meant to be just like them or better.

I wake up to music in my cell from the day room TV every morning. Puts me in a good mood and have high faith that I'll be home real soon.

They thought they could break me but I DID NOT FOLD!. In the interrogation room laughing at the detective talking about things I didn't know anything about.

Since I'm respectful and not acting like a fool, he thought he could slip something in that would implicate me to the alleged crime but I caught on and told him to show me my cell.

See they don't like when people… hold on let me rephrase that, they don't like when COLORED people know the law which is you have a right to remain silent and is exactly what I did but he also told me that half the dudes they pick up "snitch" before they can even make it to the station.

The jail isn't any better. 85% of the jail has told or is going to tell on the same person they were arrested with to receive a lesser charge. But It doesn't really make a difference because once you are in jail you're in jail until you get out. By law you're still a criminal till proven innocent.

Can I get deep with you for a second? Of course I'm not going to know what your response is or let alone know if you've made it thus far but if you have, Thank You!. Now and days I don't have much to say anymore.

I've tried to reframe from using profanity in the making of this book but screw it. What the Fuck would you do if your 10 year friend gave up on you? And I mean gave all the way up. No calls, no texts and when people ask they act like they aren't cool with you. Or tell people they aren't cool with you?

Let me tell you this now if somebody stopped messing with you than you better guarantee they're talking about you… Boosie BadAzz wasn't lying when he said it.

THE LIFE OF ME | 5

That's not even the worst part. Last year my mom planned a small get together for me and personally reached out to dude and a few other friends of mine, all was a no show but family.

Man... My mom reached out to you, why the Fuck you didn't respond? To be honest I don't care about you not showing up more than I do about you lying to my mom's like that, now that wasn't right.

We've been close for 10 long years. You know and are cool with my folks just as I am with yours. But the way you feel about somebody isn't the same way they feel about you.

Why did I call you my Day1 or brother if I'm just a homie or barely a friend when the next person asks? But some girl had the nerve to say I was trying to impress some friends just to be around. Like what's to you shorty? I've been in the streets way before I met dude and the rest of those people.

I'm the same person inside and out regardless of any situation. If anything they were using me for show's to perform together, to get hoes and to get them out of a sticky situation. If you remember where I told you I'm at while writing this... it makes sense.

If they were in my shoes they would have folded 1000%. Did I tell you after I got arrested they put me in the same block with the people I wouldn't "snitch" on to try to scare me and get me to fold and still didn't.

Like I said I'm the same person everywhere I go. And me being me I walked up to dude asking him if he wanted his one (fight) or "chop it up" while he was hiding his face with the thin blue blankets we get to sleep in. Keep in mind this is their block I'm just the newbie but buddy was still acting scared and didn't say anything until his friend who was practically in there for life says something first.

If I'm being real they were supposed to jump me but didn't and was the first two to go lock up after breakfast. Don't get me wrong I'm not the toughest nor do I want to be but when I'm paranoid and on point I'm more dangerous than I am when I'm comfortable and confident.

That's enough of that, I just wanted to vent on a street level. Not too many will understand but like I said, in my shoes they most certainly would have folded.

This year for my birthday how many wishes did I get? I can count on one hand. The previous year lots of people were vocal about celebrating me and this year… was like a ghost town. This time it was no calls, and very little post. Do you want to know the difference between my 21st birthday and my 22nd? I grew tremendously in my spirituality, mentally, physically and emotionally.

So that didn't bother me as much this year. I still took notice but it is what it is. I'm not going to go too deep into me and dude's friendship. But I basically would have did anything for bro. And you want to try and reach out now that I'm in jail after damn near a year of not hearing from you for real?. Would you want to talk…? I didn't think so.

What's done is done, I don't hate bro I still got love for dude but life goes on. I don't think y'all understand how much this pains my heart to write this. God forbid if I was to pass away I don't think I'd have enough friends to have a pallbearer.

So I'm living for me now and to tell you the truth I don't know if I'm getting out on the 29th or not but I'm not worried because God got me. God got all of us!. If you believe and give your life to God you would thank him and yourself a thousand times over. It'll all be worth it in the end.

If you made it this far I believe in you too. 2 prayers are stronger than one so my thoughts and prayers goes out to whoever reads this. And I want to be the first to tell you that better is coming! Don't quit when times get hard, just think back to why you started, go to sleep tonight at peace and ease knowing that there will be a better tomorrow!. Love.

CHAPTER

2

JAIL

Jail. Let's talk about it. What comes to mind when you think about jail or better yet, whom comes to mind? Scary right? A bad place for bad people? A practical judgement day for worldly sinners? It's all that and more but what I can say is jail isn't for anybody.

I wouldn't wish jail on my worst enemy, ever heard that saying? Well I can say that from a personal experience, except me and my enemy is locked up together. No it isn't squashed and to be honest it's no real blood shed but its still is what it is. And when they let us go they know what's up with me.

See this the thing everybody wants to be all big and bad until you get behind these walls. It can go from 0 to 100 in a blink of an eye if your not cautious. But me being on point keeps me alive in here and out in the real world.

I've been through so much from being placed in a mental hospital after losing a close friend of mine. To anger management councilors since I was young, to being in jail twice. And although those times did bother me mentally, physically and emotionally, I'm still that same person.

That same Orlando I was born to be. And what really got to me more than all of that was being left alone in a world where all I wanted was love. But got abandonment, heartache and betrayal instead.

I take all of my problems to the chin with my chest out and keep it 100% solid on my end as a man. I am a God fearing man, that prays faithfully which is why I think I am at peace while I'm behind bars. Plus another thing that plays a major factor is the fact that I'm single while I'm in here.

I don't have to stress about what my woman is doing, who she's screwing, or nothing else of that matter. I go through all of that on the outside and I'd be a fool to commit while in jail. They'll be so quick to go mess with the next man soon as you make it to booking.

But if I'm being honest this is probably the most messed up situation I've ever been in and here's why. The girl I used to be In love with is one of the main ones that's supposed to testify against me along with a person who is no longer my homie who was also in this "beef" stuff with me.

What makes matters worse is that the person who put me in here was my ex fiancée, called the states attorney to reopen the warrant out for my arrest out of spite because I left her. Would you stay with somebody who's cheating on you every time life hits you to where you lose a job or might not be able to provide for a short period of time? Crazy thing is, this isn't just a little love life situation this is real.

I didn't even tell you how I'm innocent and they just wanted to see me fail but what's really messed up is she's fucking the states attorney notice I said reopen a warrant. How do you think she got it off the first time?

I'm not going to go into detail but it's Bazar to think about right? It's like being in one of those movies where the main character is walking away from an explosion unbothered. That's me. Being at peace while my whole life is blowing up behind me but like I said I'm a God fearing man and I know that if no one else got me I know God got me and that's what is most important.

Another night has went by and I'm still strong in my faith just waiting on the day I can walk out of these doors. Plus commissary is tomorrow so I'll be eating good again until my next court date and y'all already know how I'm coming on the music side. So this new song is going to ruffle some feathers. I'll give you a hint I'm not sparing anybody (No Passes).

CHAPTER

3

RELATIONSHIPS

What is love? Is love hard? Is love patient? Is love deadly? Or is love balanced? Or is love willing and peaceful? Many things come to mind when I think about love. but what I can say is, love is all of those things and more!

Although others may fake it. Love is love and hate is hate. No matter the circumstances rather it's one sided or both. You can not say that love, when it's real, isn't one of the most strongest and power fullest thing known to man.

I'm saying all of this to say what is a relationship without love? And if you're a person of faith what is a relationship without putting the true love of God in the center of it? Nothing right?

I don't know if many can relate or not but I'm all to familiar with having neither and having my past relationships gone to shreds. After all of the hardships and trauma I've endured I learned a valuable lesson. Which was don't settle or quit when times get rough no matter who steps out on who, if it was real love in the first place that would never have happened.

I won't get into another relationship unless the love is real and she puts God first and above us so that we can build a strong family foundation we can cherish.

I've had good women in the past that I can still say to this day that I think they are great people but relationship wise it didn't workout.

Same goes for me I know I'm a good man. I just wasn't relationship compatible with a few women of my past and now I know my worth and found my purpose, my next will get nothing less than the best version of myself I can give.

I don't know everything about love but with God's help and his will, I will gain enough knowledge to install into my Children and for my legacy to be past down for generations.

Let's be honest, no one likes to be alone. The people that like to be alone are probably selfish constantly with no children and will sadly die chasing a dream missing the whole point of life.

Don't get me wrong there's nothing wrong with being alone. Even I like to be alone occasionally but at some point I want to build a family with real love continuing my last name as well as my legacy.

I want you to take in the account that I stated build instead of find. You don't find love you build a strong foundation that you and your significant other are comfortable with. It doesn't have to be based on others such as your parents, friends, celebrities and or people you desire to be like.

It can be something that only you and your partner agree upon and that's all that matters. If someone left you let them go, what is for you is for you, no man or thing can take away what and who God has for you!.

He knows the plans for your life and he knows who will accept all of you and not just the good stuff. So if someone leaves you or vise versa, it is okay. Your peace is more important trust me.

CHAPTER 4

TO MY CHILDREN

To my biological and step children I love you dearly forever and always. Some of you are old enough to understand and some of you are too young to even fathom the thought of what's going on around you.

But I want you all to know that if I hurt your feelings or did not exceed your expectations of a father I am truly sorry. All I ever wanted was a family and to be successful in life but I'm still learning and just because I did not have the love that I wanted growing up does not mean I can't show you, grow you and mold you into the best kids of my generation and yours.

You guys deserve the world man… and if it's the last thing I do I'd be damned if I don't give It to you. I want you to have the heart like I have but instead with your own flavor because each and every one of you are different in many ways.

I want you to show love, spread joy To those who you care about and to Those who need it . I want you to know that I will stand by your side through whatever and for you to also know that there's a

God who loves you and will be with you through all things in life even if there would be a time that mom and dad can't be there.

I want you to know that he is with you! I'm not where I want to be but becoming a father is one of the best things that has ever happened to me. Also has given me purpose and God has given me the strength to believe that the things I want in life will come.

Wanting so many things for my children sometimes feels like just my thoughts alone are outrageous. I had a dream that I went to this college campus, little did I know they name a part of the college after my son E'Nnogji, called Nogji lounge. Besides the name another great thing is the fact that it was an HBCU which is a major plus for our people and the black culture.

Just that small vision of a dream keeps me enthusiastic about the potential greatness of a future I can present to my children.

To E'Nnogji, me and my family love you so much. I will do anything for you son, you won't have to grow up the way I did. I will not allow you to endure the same traumas and unnecessary problems as I faced.

Your mom side I don't know much about but what I can say is me and your mom did have a good friendship bond back in high school and later on through the years you came along.

Even if it becomes something more or something less you will still be treated like the amazing son you are!

To Koah, my first born. I'm going to be honest son at first I wasn't fully sure if you were going to be mine or not based on the information your mom gave me in the beginning.

Your mom will take great care of you, as will I. You are my world son and if it wasn't for you I wouldn't be on this earth. You gave me purpose. A new reason to want to live again and for that I owe it all to you.

Do me a favor and take it easy on your mom, it's her first time. Regardless of me and your mother's situation you will get everything you want and need to be successful in this life and in the next.

I came from a family that showed favoritism to certain individuals and I've seen the damages as a reflection because of it. I will not allow that same thing to happen with you and your brother, the world is yours we're just living in it.

To Dreyah, I want to start this off by saying daddy so sorry baby. The problems me and your mom had affected my appearance during the terms of pregnancy.

I will have great stories to tell and also bad ones… but when the time is right you will know them all.

For the concerns as far as your mom and I, things had to come to an end. Your mom put me in a bad place and did things I cannot forgive her for.

After I previously forgave her for the things that she did throughout our relationship. She allowed the world to destroy us as I allowed her to destroy me spiritually, emotionally and mentally which took a major toll on me in the long run.

I can keep going but I'm just going to stop here and leave it at that. I can say I did love her and her family regardless of any situation but I'm sorry to tell you that the times of rekindling are over with for me.

It's nothing against her family because I love them as if they were my own but it's too much pain and suffering from everything and everyone in Carbondale.

I'm wiping my hands from it all. Now I only want my children in my life and peace. I'm cool on being in a relationship for a while and while everyone else is playing catch up or plotting on their next get back against me I will continue to focus on my future.

I said all of this to say, NO ONE WILL EVER TAKE ME AWAY FROM YOU AGAIN! I'm going to give you the world baby girl and you deserve nothing but the best. I promise it'll be just that.

Me and you are the only two people in my family with this last name and I want you to continue the family legacy that I create from love, care, excitement, teachings and above all the powerful will and love of God.

You will know God and grow to care for him through love and compassion. Same as I did. I love you so much baby girl, daddy got you for life princess!

To my children that did not make it into this world I am so sorry my beautiful babies but God had other plans for you. I love you with all my heart.

CHAPTER

5

FORGIVENESS

How much is forgiveness worth to you? Is it worth more than an apology? Or whatever the error was fixed? I think forgiveness played a crucial part throughout the years to were I don't want anymore mishaps in my life although it may be inevitable.

Have you ever unintentionally hurt someone? And I mean you tried your damnedest not to… do you want to know why that happened? Because your life tends to move in the direction of your strongest thoughts.

With you being so focused on it not happening you could miss out on the potential of it happening which could leave you in a state of shock or a distraught feeling.

Even though your intentions may be pure, no one will believe you've had good intentions from the start. Sometimes being forgiven isn't enough because you're still left with an admission of guilt no matter how big or how small the situation is.

The feeling of being guilty will eat you alive just as much as stress and or going through a stage of depression would. The human race is known to be unforgiving, hold grudges, seek revenge, hold resentment towards one another and the list can go on.

How many times have you tried to fix something and throughout all your efforts you still failed at every attempt to make a situation better but only to make matters worse? It's because that person has yet to forgive you and doesn't plan to no time soon.

And you know what… it's okay. Sometimes you have to give people their space and allow them to breathe and heal. What I like to say is let go and let God. If it's meant to be he will allow them to find it in their hearts to forgive you. If not then it's okay to move on with your life with a learning experience to reflect on.

Should I forgive her? Should I forgive her for letting it drag for this long? Or for she being the reason I lost another good job again!? Or me missing out on my college classes, missing my freedom, not being able to handle my responsibilities, and miss out on countless opportunities to fulfill my dreams and passions… should I?

I ask myself those questions continuously. Sometimes without reason but I can assure you I have a damn good reason to. I can admit that I don't give others room to grow at times because of anger and or how hurtful the situation may be. But what I can say is I do apologize when I'm wrong and it would also make me a hypocrite not to accept the change in others when I would like for them to acknowledge the changes I've made over time.

Although it may be hard, change is most certainly needed whether it be for you or the other party. As for my situation I think the changes I needed to make for myself was well overdue along with me accepting people for who they are or seeing a situation for what it is and not for what I want it to be.

I can forgive her but I wont forget. And if Dreyah Is real and is mine, which in my mind she is but you never can be too sure with the women of this generation, then I don't have to be with her mother. She will always be apart of the affects had on my life good or bad all the while being thankful for our situation to know what I needed to do for my life.

I would also like to give thanks to our lord and savior Jesus Christ for allowing me to acknowledge my strengths and weaknesses. And for giving me wisdom to know that joy will come in the morning.

The Life you want will be given to you as long as you stay steadfast in your faith.

CHAPTER

6

LETTING GO AND MOVING ON

I don't know where I should start. From losing friends to losing family and the life I built for myself. On top of that being put behind bars on two counts of aggravated gun charges. To being told on by someone who I claimed to have loved not to mention just had a new born back in July that is now supposed to be 2 months old. Who just came out and told me that her and the man who reopened my case aka the states attorney, had sexual relations and is now pregnant all in a short span of a month.

So no, I don't know where I should start and throughout all the things that transpired in my life I can say this with 100% certainty this tops the cake.

It's almost hard to believe that my body is at peak shape with a liver that's going bad and I've had the knees of a 40 year old man since I can remember. My heart is numb and to say my emotions are high is a complete understatement.

The only thing I have left is my faith. Sometimes it feels like I barely have that but prayer keeps me reassured that it's still there. There's more than half The world that I have yet to explore than for me to be worried about little ole Carbondale and the miserable people in it.

I won't take away the fact that I do need help. And I know what you're thinking, "haven't you been down this counseling route before"? Yes I have but I believe that If I could find one more good one they'll set me straight one last time.

This situation has made me so infuriated That I don't think I can describe how I feel or the emotions rushing through my body at this point in time. All I can say is I'm done. I'm done with it all.

I mean I don't even want to be me anymore, I quit. I give in. Call a time out or something! This isn't right at all… I'm not saying my life doesn't has it's perks and moments, it just doesn't last long enough for me to enjoy the wins.

I can accomplish a lot of things when I'm by myself but when you're tied down to family, relationships and even friendships eventually you would get tired. Everybody would want a piece of you so much to the point you won't have anything left for yourself.

I'm not one to blame the likes of others for the things and events that partake in my time on this earth. I know I need to hold those who are at fault accountable, I tend to forgive because of the forgiving heart I was lucky to be blessed with although at times feels like a curse.

I hate to feel like a burden to anyone's life but if I continue to be there for everyone in their life, I'm going to miss out on enjoying my own.

I won't necessarily stop helping others completely but I will start putting my needs for my life first and now that I have children who need and depend on me, I have to do what's best for them along with myself. Nothing else matters now.

My priority goes to the family I create, I've already wasted 22 years of my life on doing for others, I will now live by my means and by the will of our heavenly father.

CHAPTER 7

A NEWER ME

PART ONE

Turning over a new leaf is mandatory in life. Think about it as if a reptile sheds it's skin or the way caterpillars turn into butterflies. Change is necessary.

Don't get me wrong I know what I've been talking about in the previous chapters even if I was jus writing out my thoughts and feelings at the time. I did love her an I know she loved me too before all of the drama.

She's making all of the write changes that she needed to make not only for herself but for the sake of the bond we once shared. I can for surely see the growth and I can honestly say I'm proud of her.

We've been through too much to let go in seconds what took months to build. We've won together and we've loss together. And we're a hell of a team when we put our best foot's forward.

If I'm being honest this is where real love starts. It's when the feelings end. When you think you've done all you can do and your start to become numb to the situation.

She was there for me while I was incarcerated. Now rather it was because she felt guilty for what she did or she genuinely cared I don't know but she was there to put money on my books and to pick up the phone when I'd call.

My family did their part too but of course it didn't last long nor am I mad at them about it. As far as friends go nobody did anything, not a visit… nothing. It's nobody's fault I was in that predicament but mine so I'm willing to look past that.

I think we can move past this and put it all behind us to create something so strong that nothing could break us. Besides who wants to start over and potentially go through more problems with the next person when we can both fix our errors and overcome this life changing moment.

I won't rush into it though it was just a thought. I still need to do what's best for me and my life accomplishing the overall goals I set for myself. I'm going to be about it instead of just speaking on it and I'm going to do what it takes to get it done.

As a man all you have is your word, what you can provide and the code you live by, so if you don't stick to your word what good is it worth…? Exactly!

I started this book when I was in jail and now that I am out a lot has changed since then. Just like the way I started off with this chapter, I regret what I said about her.

She lied about having my baby and brought someone else's baby up to the jail to visit me with her almost everyday as well as to the court house the day I got released.

I wasn't out for a good 5 days and here I am met with some problems. It started out with the argument about her still being on her sneaky ways and continuous lying spree. But you know what they say once a snake always a snake.

Then all of a sudden there was a knock on the door, no one answered due to the fact we were in mid argument. Then the second knock, this time it came from the bedroom window. "Marion Police Department open up", she fly's to the front door while I'm standing in the bed room holding the baby I believed to be my daughter. So I was told…

What happened next was so traumatizing and mind boggling that I was too calm for my own good. As I walked outside to see what was going on, with the thought in the back of my mind that they were there for me, knowing I jus got out a few days ago kept me on my toes.

You wouldn't believe what the officer told me along with the DCFS (Department of Children and Family Services) worker said out loud to us. She stated that the girl I was with, took someone else's baby trying to convince me that the child was my daughter.

In my mind I didn't think much of it at first because I was holding said baby. And the fact of what I went through for this baby situation alone. What stood out to me was the fact that they said there was no record of her having a baby at SIH or at Saint Louis Children's hospital.

And during her appointments there was no evidence that she was ever even pregnant!. Man my heart dropped to my ass… at that point I was ready to go right upside her head all because she lied. About EVERYTHING!

Not even just to me but to everybody about being pregnant and having stage 4 leukemia cancer. What the hell is wrong with this lady!? She put me through all this and had y'all on her side about our relationship and now this?.

But I get it people don't care about what they did or what was said because of this manipulating girl. Y'all don't owe me nothing. I'm going to end this short, after they took the baby out of my arms that night they end up taking the baby to the hospital as one of their procedures.

Come to find out the baby that I believe was my daughter due to what I was told was in fact a baby boy dressed in girls clothing. This whole time she's been playing dress up wit someone else's son posing as a baby girl to convince me that was our daughter she was supposed to have back in July and been at it since I was incarcerated.

And before you say why didn't you just changed the baby's diapers you would have found out sooner… Hence that was part of the argument we had before they showed up and took the baby.

But Let me guess that's my fault too right? I'm made out to be the bad guy in everyone's story. This type of thing is what you would see in a movie or would be featured in a life time segment. But It is what it is, never in my right mind did I ever think this could have possibly turned out the way it did.

If I acted off of emotions I would not see the light of day ever again. I'm a man at the end of the day I'm supposed to handle this and take that to the chin and move on with life.

Screw that!. If I don't get that Mental help that I need I'm going to go insane. I was on the right path before I got arrested just for her and whoever else that was behind this do me like that!? I am at a loss for words.

The day I got arrested I had my son with me after I just left a funeral for my great aunt that recently passed away, that's the second one within a couple of months apart. She got arrested that day at the park but didn't even make it to the station. How Ironic is that? That they let her go just to turn around and pick me up on a case that has been closed due to lack of evidence.

This isn't right not one bit. I feel like I wasn't mad enough, I was too calm for my own liking but I know me; and the evil side would have had me spending the rest of my life in prison.

People knew and chose not to say anything including her family. The whole world has problems and I don't want to be apart of it anymore. I quit!.

To be continued…

PART TWO

I was at a loss for words. I mean why go to these extreme lengths? I know some folks viewpoints and opinions are different than others, that one may ask themselves this question as in what did he do to her to make her result into this craziness? Which I completely understand if that's you're take on all of this.

Don't get me wrong I did not make this book to bash anybody only to share my thoughts, feelings and experiences that I face over the course of a year and a few months. I can admit I was the problem at times… I would let my emotions get the best of me and would leave out of anger in response to when I felt disrespected or if I would not be able to voice my opinion. And at times it was almost like I had to pick an choose between my kids that I didn't know where mine at the time or her.

It's messed up to put a person in that type of position but when it came down to my sons I showed up when I needed to the most. Back off in march when my first son was born I was not able to be there during the time of birth because I had a warrant out for my arrest, but I still managed to make a way to show up for him a couple days after.

Less than a month later in April my youngest son was born. I wasn't there during the delivery process but I was there shortly after he arrived. Which turned out to be short lived due to arguments and misunderstandings. I was on the side of my kids but also on the side of my relationship solely out of respect, I invited her with me to the hospital to wait in the waiting room while I go see my son and handle whatever else that needed to be taken care of as far as me being the father.

When people are still stuck in their ways or are still stuck on how a person(s) treated them in the past they tend to jump right into another relationship not truly healing from past experiences. I say that because I used to be that way and I understand the hardship of trying to heal from situations when you're the only one left stuck there and everyone else has moved on. But until you take time out for self, you will not be able to heal yourself properly or move on in life the way God intended it to be.

If you could give advice to your younger self what would it be? I would say don't live to please everybody. It's okay to be selfish for the things you want and deserve. Some people will love you for who you are and others will love you for what you can do for them and when you have nothing left to give they will leave you without hesitation.

I would also tell my younger self stay on the porch… don't jump. Finish college all the way through, and don't look up to your brothers bad side and your father's name in the streets. Be your own man which I know you don't have a problem with doing but at least find other people that are more encouraging to look up to that's not surrounded by death and jail sentences.

And one more thing don't make that move that you will regret for the rest of your life. I know why you did it, and I understand where you're heart was at… but just know it's going to lead to jail time. Even though it was for a fight and you only had to spend a couple weekends in there that's not the problem. My concern is your mental state when you found out you had to go and you couldn't be there for your first ever child's doctors appointment.

Many didn't know this, but before I had my oldest son Koah I lost a baby that would have meant the world to me. Not only because that baby would have been my first but also because of the person I was going to have him or her by. I was devastated when I got that call the same day I got released from jail.

I just wanted to be there for her even though she was trying to stay strong for me I didn't care about my feelings at that time. But from that moment on I told her " I got you for life". And I meant that. I try to look at every negative situation as a positive in most cases. And after I mourned the loss of that baby I looked to the skies with tears of joy because I knew I had to take a loss to birth what God really had in store for me which was my two handsome boys E'Nnogji and Koah.

I don't live with regrets. Anything that I went through was either a lesson or a blessing. Living with regrets does nothing but causes you to live with a constant level of stress, unnecessary worrying, pressure from something that doesn't hold any weight in the current environment you're living in now and it also can cause you to fear your past instead of embracing it then moving on to live in the present moment.

CHAPTER 8

FAMILY

What would you do with out family? What role do you play in your family tree? I want you to ask yourself this question, what is more important to you? The family you come from? Or the family you create? From a personal standpoint I would say both.

I do have a lot of un-healed pain and past trauma from the family I come from. But I refuse to give up on what potential my family actually has to become something great in the near future.

My parents have the best friendship/ co-parenting bond they've ever had in my entire existence. They are also willing to compromise and sacrifice anything for the greater good of my future as well as for my two son's.

I can proudly say they are both ecstatic to be grandparents. I didn't have the best up bringing but I am thankful for my parents. Being there through every trial and error that my mother faced, to seeing her at her lowest of lows and highest of highs.

That lady is strong! With whatever was thrown her way I never saw her complain. I was there to wipe her tears when no one else was there or bothered to check in. I feel like I'm a gift from God to her and to show her that if no one else is there, I will always be forever and always!

This is personal from my heart. To my mom, I love you and I apologize for all of those times I caused you pain. And all of those late night worries I understand why things happened the way they did and what you had to do as a mother.

And for that reason alone is why I will never not appreciate you and give you the flowers you deserve. It is important to appreciate what you have while you still can because there are some who are less fortunate to still be able to call just to hear their mothers voice.

Regardless of who's right or who's wrong, don't let the effects of your relationship cause you to lose sight of something you can't get back.! In the wise words of J. Cole, love yours!

To my first baby mother, you have a bright future ahead of you with a heart of gold. I think you needed our handsome baby boy Koah in your life. Many don't know your story but I'm thankful to get to know that side of you and to see how passionate you are about the things you want in your life.

We don't argue and needless to say we do have our moments where we disagree with one another but I think the best thing for us to do in this situation is to stay friends and have the best co-parenting bond. That when we come together for our son no one would be able to tell the difference.

To protect our son, I feel as though this is best for the greater good of our child. It's a lot of hurt that you're not healed from when it comes to me and for that I apologize. It's no point in trying to see who's wrong or who's right about the situation, the point is we're family now and I will do anything for the sake of our son.

I don't know if you'll come back around or not. But we both have valid reasons to feel the way we do. Whatever the outcome may be, you know what it means to me to be a father. And how important it is for me to be in my sons life.

I will never stop fighting for my son. I will go to war with the world, hell... even you if I have to. No it shouldn't have to come down to that but if this is where this road leads to, then so be it. It's all love though, I'm thankful to have met half of your family. Our son is lucky to have both parties involved.

To my second baby mother, E'Nnogji came at the right time for me. I'm grateful for our precious baby boy. Both of my son's changed my life for the better but it's something about E'Nnogji that reminds me of my father as well as myself.

He will have a different but yet better childhood than I've ever had and I know we both can agree when I say that. But I want to designate this part to you. I like the bond we share. The way we're raising our kid is damn near flawless.

I know we can be something special and build our family as we both envisioned. You bring the right type of peace that I need in my life. I don't have to look over my shoulder when I'm with you and our son. We enjoy each other's company so much that I only see how things can go right with us in the future.

Most importantly you kept it real from jump. You never lied. And that is important to me more than you know! I can talk to you about anything that's on my mind without having to bite my tongue knowing there will be no judgment.

I have nothing but the up most respect for you. Even when I make you mad we can recover from any situation. What I really like is the fact that you don't keep E'Nnogji away from me and you allow me to be the father that I need and want to be.

I also like how you don't feel out of place when I bring you around my family. When you're comfortable I'm comfortable. You held me down when I was in jail, answered every phone call, if I needed to vent you was there and always let me talk to my son to keep me strong while I was away.

The way you filled that visitation list up once you finally figured out how it worked I knew from that point you wasn't playing any games when it came down to me and my son. I commend you for that. And you for surely stand on business when it comes to ole girl by winning the restraining order battle regardless of the connection she has.

I can't forget to mention the physical battles you win every time she tries to pick or cause you harm. We all have our flaws but I don't see yours. Based off of the loyalty and respect alone, I'm holding you close and we'll work on the vulnerable stages as we go and grow.

My life is complicated but yet meaningful. I do miss some folks from my past and I hope you can see my growth. Lord knows I mean well. God hasn't given up on me so why should I? My future is still very bright and if you doubt me, thank you! That adds fuel to the fire of my motivation.

I'm finally free. Although I'm on probation for 2 years I'm still free of a jail cell. I moved to a new state with the intent of finding myself again. I love my hometown it brought a lot of great memories but they show me more hate than love.

I don't care to be liked. I'm in my own little world most of the time anyway. To keep my peace I will stay out of their face because I know how far I'm going to take it once I react.

My story started off rough, but it has a good encouraging ending to it though it is far from over. My brother got released two days after I did. He now lives far away from Carbondale working his butt off for the life he finally gets to live and enjoy while taking care of his two year old son.

Congrats on your new promotion bro! My middle sister made a full 360 recovery after being in the hospital and quit drinking not quite fully but enough to realize that she doesn't have to over drink to mask her pain.

If you've dealt with the same struggle as my sister it's better for you to face your problems instead of trying to find coping mechanisms to hide the pain.

I'm proud of my sister and I'm proud of whoever else reads this that share a similar struggle. Keep going, you matter!

To my oldest sister, keep doing what you're doing. You've found a way to make life work for you and if you're happy then I'm happy. Of course we're going to fight it's what siblings do but that doesn't mean I love you any less.

With that being said, that concludes this journey. Who knows maybe I'll come back with a part two and tell different sides of the story through their perspective. I think that'll put an interesting spin on things.

But for now take with you what you've learned, share if you can relate, understand what it is like for a person of my stature to deal with the adversities and the challenges I face day to day. I Hope my story can help you grow and move on from mistakes the past you made. I want you to wake up everyday knowing that you are that much closer to your dreams and goals, never give up!

www.ingramcontent.com/pod-product-compliance
Lightning Source LLC
Chambersburg PA
CBHW031436040426
42444CB00006B/845